DEPARTMENT OF JUSTICE

**FREQUENTLY ASKED QUESTIONS
ABOUT THE ANTITRUST DIVISION'S LENIENCY PROGRAM
AND MODEL LENIENCY LETTERS
Originally Published November 19, 2008
Update Published January 17, 2017**

The Antitrust Division's Leniency Program[1] allows corporations and individuals involved in antitrust crimes to self-report and avoid criminal convictions and resulting fines and incarceration. The first corporate or individual conspirator to confess participation in an antitrust crime, fully cooperate with the Division, and meet all other conditions that the Corporate Leniency Policy or the Leniency Policy for Individuals specifies receives leniency for the reported antitrust crime.

Several Division speeches explain the program and its requirements,[2] and describe what a prospective applicant can expect when deciding to approach the Division and apply for leniency. Model conditional leniency letters for both corporate and individual applicants are publicly available and show how the conditional leniency agreement between the Division and an applicant is memorialized.[3] The answers to these Frequently Asked Questions restate much of the information that is already available in the speeches and model letters. They are a comprehensive and updated resource that provides guidance with respect to common issues that leniency applicants encounter under the Division's Corporate Leniency Policy and Leniency Policy for Individuals. These Frequently Asked Questions address: 1) leniency application procedures; 2) the criteria for receiving leniency under the Corporate Leniency Policy; 3) the criteria for receiving leniency under the Leniency Policy for Individuals; 4) the conditional leniency letter; 5) the potential revocation of conditional leniency and the final unconditional leniency letter; and 6) confidentiality for leniency applicants.

The Leniency Program's success is in part due to the Division's consideration of the views and incorporation of the input of the private bar and business community. The Division continues to solicit suggestions on how to keep the program transparent, predictable, and fair. These Frequently Asked Questions are therefore periodically updated, with a new date on the title page identifying the current version.

---

[1] The Division first implemented a leniency program in 1978. It issued its Corporate Leniency Policy in 1993, which substantially revised the program, and a Leniency Policy for Individuals in 1994. The Division's Corporate Leniency Policy and Leniency Policy for Individuals are available at https://www.justice.gov/atr/leniency-program.

[2] Speeches about the Leniency Program are available at https://www.justice.gov/atr/leniency-program.

[3] The model conditional leniency letters are available at https://www.justice.gov/atr/leniency-program.

I. Leniency Application Procedures

Application Contact Information

1. *Who does counsel for a potential applicant contact to apply for leniency?*

The Division's Deputy Assistant Attorney General for Criminal Enforcement ("Criminal DAAG") reviews and evaluates all requests for leniency, including the scope of any leniency marker extended.[4] An applicant's counsel should contact the Criminal DAAG or the Director of Criminal Enforcement at 202-514-3543 to request a marker. Marker requests made to one of the Division's criminal offices will be forwarded immediately to the Criminal DAAG for determination about the availability of a marker.

Securing a Marker

The Division understands that when corporate counsel first obtains indications of a possible criminal antitrust violation, authoritative personnel for the company may not have sufficient information to know for certain whether the corporation has engaged in such a violation, an admission of which is required to obtain a conditional leniency letter.[5] Counsel should understand, however, that time is of the essence in making a leniency application. The Division grants only one corporate leniency per conspiracy, and in applying for leniency, the company is in a race with its co-conspirators and possibly its own employees who may also be preparing to apply for individual leniency. On a number of occasions, the second company to inquire about a leniency application has been beaten by a prior applicant by only a matter of hours. Thus, the Division has established a marker system to hold an applicant's place in the line for leniency while the applicant gathers more information to support its leniency application.

2. *What is a marker, and how is it used in the leniency application process?*

The Division frequently gives a leniency applicant a "marker" for a finite period of time to hold its place at the front of the line for leniency while counsel gathers additional information through an internal investigation to perfect the client's leniency

---

[4] Note that the Corporate Leniency Policy, which was issued in 1993, states that the Director of Operations reviews corporate leniency applications, and the Leniency Policy for Individuals, which was issued in 1994, states that the Deputy Assistant Attorney General for Litigation reviews individual leniency applications. Both of the leniency policies were written before the Division created the Criminal DAAG position and gave that position oversight of the Division's criminal enforcement program, including the Division's Leniency Program.

[5] *See* Question 5.

application. While the marker is in effect, no other company can "leapfrog" over the applicant that has the marker.

To obtain a marker, counsel must: (1) report that he or she has uncovered some information or evidence indicating that his or her client has engaged in a criminal antitrust violation; (2) disclose the general nature of the conduct discovered; (3) identify the industry, product, or service involved in terms that are specific enough to allow the Division to determine whether leniency is still available and to protect the marker for the applicant; and (4) identify the client. As noted above, when corporate counsel first obtains indications of a possible criminal antitrust violation, authoritative personnel for the company may not have sufficient information to enable them to admit definitively to such a violation. While confirmation of a criminal antitrust violation is not required at the marker stage, in order to receive a marker, counsel must report that he or she has uncovered information or evidence suggesting a possible criminal antitrust violation, e.g., price fixing, bid rigging, capacity restriction, or allocation of markets, customers, or sales or production volumes. It is not enough for counsel to state merely that the client has received a grand jury subpoena or has been searched during a Division investigation and that counsel wants a marker to investigate whether the client has committed a criminal antitrust violation.

Because companies are urged to seek leniency at the first indication of wrongdoing, the evidentiary standard for obtaining a marker is relatively low, particularly in situations where the Division is not already investigating the wrongdoing. For example, if an attorney gave a compliance presentation and after the presentation an employee reported to the attorney a conversation the employee had overheard about his employer's potential price-fixing activities, this information would be sufficient to obtain a marker if one is available. However, when the Division is already in possession of information about the illegal activity, a more detailed report of the antitrust crime may be required to determine the availability and appropriate scope of a marker. Regardless of whether the Division already has information about the illegal activity, as noted above, counsel should request a marker as soon as possible and can discuss with the Division whether more detailed information is needed to secure his or her client's place at the front of the line for leniency.

In some cases, an identification of the industry may be sufficient for the Division to determine whether leniency is available. In many cases, however, it is necessary to identify specific products or services, other companies involved in the conspiracy, or the identity or location of affected customers, for the Division to determine whether leniency is available and the proper scope of the marker.

A marker is provided for a finite period. The length of time an applicant is given to perfect its leniency application is based on factors such as the location and number of company employees counsel needs to interview, the amount and location of documents counsel needs to review, and whether the Division already has an ongoing investigation at the time the marker is requested. A 30-day period for an initial marker is common, particularly in situations where the Division is not yet investigating the wrongdoing. If necessary, the marker may be extended at the Division's discretion for an additional finite period as long as the applicant demonstrates it is making a good-faith effort to complete its application in a timely manner.

II. Corporate Leniency Criteria

3. What are the criteria for obtaining corporate leniency and is corporate leniency available both before and after an investigation has begun?

Leniency is available for corporations either before or after a Division investigation has begun. The Corporate Leniency Policy includes two types of leniency: Type A and Type B. Type A Leniency is available only before the Division has received any information about the activity being reported from any source, while Type B Leniency is available even after the Division has received information about the activity. Detailed below are the criteria for each type of leniency.

Leniency Before an Investigation Has Begun ("Type A Leniency")

Leniency will be granted to a corporation reporting illegal antitrust activity before an investigation has begun if the following six conditions are met:

1) At the time the corporation comes forward to report the illegal activity, the Division has not received information about the illegal activity being reported from any other source;

2) The corporation, upon its discovery of the illegal activity being reported, took prompt and effective action to terminate its part in the activity;

3) The corporation reports the wrongdoing with candor and completeness and provides full, continuing and complete cooperation to the Division throughout the investigation;

4) The confession of wrongdoing is truly a corporate act, as opposed to isolated confessions of individual executives or officials;

5) Where possible, the corporation makes restitution to injured parties; and

6) The corporation did not coerce another party to participate in the illegal activity and clearly was not the leader in, or originator of, the activity.

If the corporation does not meet all six of the Type A Leniency conditions, it may still qualify for leniency if it meets the conditions of Type B Leniency.

Alternative Requirements for Leniency ("Type B Leniency")

A company will be granted leniency even after the Division has received information—such as from an anonymous complainant, a private civil action, or a press report—about the illegal antitrust activity, whether this is before or after an investigation has begun, if the following conditions are met:

1) The corporation is the first one to come forward and qualify for leniency with respect to the illegal activity being reported;

2) The Division, at the time the corporation comes in, does not yet have evidence against the company that is likely to result in a sustainable conviction;

3) The corporation, upon its discovery of the illegal activity being reported, took prompt and effective action to terminate its part in the activity;

4) The corporation reports the wrongdoing with candor and completeness and provides full, continuing and complete cooperation that advances the Division in its investigation;

5) The confession of wrongdoing is truly a corporate act, as opposed to isolated confessions of individual executives or officials;

6) Where possible, the corporation makes restitution to injured parties; and

7) The Division determines that granting leniency would not be unfair to others, considering the nature of the illegal activity, the confessing corporation's role in it, and when the corporation comes forward.

The "First-in-the-Door" Requirement

4. *Can more than one company qualify for leniency?*

No. Under both Type A Leniency and Type B Leniency, only the first qualifying corporation may be granted leniency for a particular antitrust conspiracy. Condition 1 of Type A Leniency requires that the Division has not yet received information about the illegal antitrust activity being reported from any other source, and Condition 1 of Type B Leniency requires that the company is the first to come forward and qualify for leniency. Under the policy that only the first qualifying corporation receives conditional leniency,[6] there have been dramatic differences in the disposition of the criminal liability of corporations whose respective leniency applications to the Division were very close in

---

[6] See Question 26 for a discussion of the conditional nature of the Division's leniency letters.

time. Therefore, companies have a huge incentive to make a leniency application as quickly as possible.

Criminal Violation

5. *Does a leniency applicant have to admit to a criminal violation of the antitrust laws before receiving a conditional leniency letter?*

Yes. The Division's leniency policies were established for corporations and individuals "reporting their illegal antitrust activity," and the policies protect leniency recipients from criminal conviction. Thus, the applicant must admit its participation in a criminal antitrust violation involving price fixing, bid rigging, capacity restriction, or allocation of markets, customers, or sales or production volumes, before it will receive a conditional leniency letter. Applicants that have not engaged in criminal violations of the antitrust laws have no need to receive leniency protection from a criminal violation and will not qualify for leniency through the Leniency Program.

When the model corporate conditional leniency letter was first drafted, the Division did not employ a marker system. Thus, companies received conditional leniency letters far earlier in the process, often before the company had an opportunity to conduct an internal investigation. However, the Division's practice has changed over time. The Division now employs a marker system, and the Division provides the company with an opportunity to investigate thoroughly its own conduct. While the applicant may not be able to confirm that it committed a criminal antitrust violation when it seeks and receives a marker, by the end of the marker process, before it is provided a conditional leniency letter, it should be in a position to admit to its participation in a criminal violation of the Sherman Act. The Division may also insist on interviews with key executives of the applicant who were involved in the violation before issuing the conditional leniency letter. A company that argues that an agreement to fix prices, rig bids, restrict capacity, or allocate markets might be inferred from its conduct but that cannot produce any employees who will admit that the company entered into such an agreement generally has not made a sufficient admission of a criminal antitrust violation to be eligible for leniency. A company that, for whatever reason, is not able or willing to admit to its participation in a criminal antitrust conspiracy is not eligible for leniency.[7]

---

[7] Before the original version of these Frequently Asked Questions were issued in November 2008, the model conditional leniency letters referred to the conduct being reported as "*possible* [. . . price fixing, bid rigging, market allocation] or other conduct violative of Section 1 of the Sherman Act." (emphasis added). Because applicants must report a criminal violation of the antitrust laws before receiving a conditional leniency letter, the word "possible" has been deleted from the model letter, and a reference to "or other conduct constituting a criminal violation of Section 1 of the Sherman Act" has been added to the model corporate and individual conditional leniency letters, which are available at https://www.justice.gov/atr/leniency-program.

Non-Antitrust Crimes

6. *How does the Division's Leniency Program apply to non-antitrust crimes?*

In the model conditional leniency letter, the Antitrust Division commits to not prosecute a qualifying leniency applicant for the antitrust violation it reports or for acts or offenses integral to that violation. For example, conduct integral to the reported antitrust violation, such as mailing or emailing conspiratorially set bids, may itself constitute another offense such as mail or wire fraud. The Division's model conditional leniency letter provides that the Division will not prosecute a qualifying leniency applicant for these additional offenses "committed prior to the date of [the] letter in furtherance of" the reported antitrust violation.[8]

The conditional leniency letter, however, binds only the Antitrust Division; it does not bind other federal or state prosecuting agencies, including other components of the Department of Justice. The Division's Leniency Program does not protect applicants from criminal prosecution by other prosecuting agencies for offenses other than Sherman Act violations. For example, a leniency applicant that bribed foreign public officials in violation of the Foreign Corrupt Practices Act receives no protection from prosecution by any other prosecuting agency, regardless of whether the bribes were also made in furtherance of the reported antitrust violation. In addition, a leniency application does not discharge prior reporting obligations to other prosecuting agencies, nor does it insulate the leniency applicant from the consequences of violating earlier agreements not to commit crimes.

It has been the Antitrust Division's experience that other prosecuting agencies do not use other criminal statutes to do an end-run around leniency. At the same time, leniency applicants should not expect to use the Leniency Program to avoid accountability for non-antitrust crimes. Not every conspiracy among competitors amounts to an antitrust crime. And not every fraud that an applicant commits while engaged in an antitrust crime is committed in furtherance of that crime.

Leniency applicants with exposure for both antitrust and non-antitrust crimes should report all crimes to the relevant prosecuting agencies. Under the Department's Principles of Federal Prosecution of Business Organizations, self-reporting is one factor that federal prosecuting agencies consider when making charging decisions. A list of factors that will be weighed in deciding whether to prosecute a company can be found at U.S. Attorneys' Manual 9-28.300 ("U.S.A.M.").[9] These Principles recognize special

---

[8] Model Corp. Conditional Leniency Letter ¶ 3; Model Individual Conditional Leniency Letter ¶ 3.

[9] Offices of U.S. Attorneys, *U.S. Attorneys' Manual* 9-28.000, https://www.justice.gov/usam/usam-9-28000-principles-federal-prosecution-business-organizations.

policy goals and incentive programs regarding antitrust violations, among other offenses, and note the Antitrust Division's "firm policy . . . that amnesty is available only to the first corporation to make full disclosure to the government."[10]

Scope of Markers and Leniency

7. *If during the course of its internal investigation, an applicant discovers and reports evidence that the anticompetitive activity was broader or narrower than originally reported, for example, in terms of its geographic scope or the number of products involved, can the scope of the applicant's marker or leniency protection change?*

Yes. Companies often request markers before completing their internal investigations. When the Division gives a marker to a company, this secures the company's place in line as the first and only leniency applicant. The scope of the marker is tailored to the facts that the applicant proffers at the time it requests it. Because the applicant must proffer facts indicating its participation in a criminal antitrust conspiracy, the scope of the marker is coextensive with the scope of the conspiracy that the applicant reports.

Because it uses a marker system, the Division often learns from an applicant, or its employees as part of the corporate confession, that the scope of the conspiracy is broader than the applicant originally reported. For example, an applicant's executives might provide evidence as part of the corporate confession showing that the anticompetitive activity was broader in terms of its geographic scope or the number of products involved in the conspiracy than originally reported. So long as the applicant has not tried to conceal the conduct, is providing truthful, full, continuing, and complete cooperation, and can meet the criteria for leniency on the broader activity, the marker or conditional leniency letter will be tailored to the scope of the conspiracy reported.

Occasionally, the investigation of a conspiracy that a leniency applicant reports reveals that the conspiracy is narrower than the applicant originally reported. The marker or conditional leniency letter will accordingly be tailored to the scope of the conspiracy that the evidence supports, so long as the applicant's original report was made in good faith, the applicant is providing truthful, full, continuing, and complete cooperation, and the applicant can meet the leniency criteria.

Sometimes while attempting to perfect a marker, an applicant will discover conduct that constitutes a separate conspiracy. In this case, if a marker is available for the separate conspiracy, the applicant can request another marker. If the Division gives the applicant the new marker, like all markers, it will be tailored to the facts that the applicant proffers when requesting it.

---

[10] U.S.A.M. 9-28.400, 9-28.800, and 9-28.900.

"Leniency Plus"

8. *If a company is under investigation for one antitrust conspiracy but is too late to obtain leniency for that conspiracy, can it receive additional credit for substantial assistance in its plea agreement for that conspiracy by reporting its involvement in a separate antitrust conspiracy?*

Yes. Many of the Division's investigations result from evidence developed during an investigation of a completely separate conspiracy. This pattern has led the Division to take a proactive approach to attracting leniency applications by encouraging subjects and targets of investigations to consider whether they may qualify for leniency in other markets where they compete. For example, consider the following hypothetical fact pattern:

> *As a result of cooperation received pursuant to a leniency application in the widgets market, a grand jury is investigating the other four producers in that market, including XYZ, Inc., for their participation in an international cartel. As part of its internal investigation, XYZ, Inc., uncovers information of its executives' participation not only in a widgets cartel but also in a separate conspiracy in the sprockets market. The government has not detected the sprockets cartel because the leniency applicant was not a competitor in that market and no other investigation has disclosed the cartel activity. XYZ, Inc. is interested in cooperating with the Division's widgets investigation pursuant to a plea agreement and seeking leniency by reporting its participation in the sprockets conspiracy. Assuming XYZ, Inc. qualifies for leniency with respect to the sprockets conspiracy, what credit for substantial assistance can XYZ, Inc. receive?*

Assuming that XYZ, Inc. qualifies for leniency with respect to the sprockets conspiracy and provides truthful, full, continuing, and complete cooperation with the Division's investigation into the widgets conspiracy, XYZ, Inc. can obtain what the Division refers to as "Leniency Plus." The Division would grant leniency to XYZ, Inc. in the sprockets investigation, meaning that XYZ, Inc. would pay zero dollars in fines for its role in the sprockets conspiracy and none of its current[11] directors, officers and employees who admitted to the Division their knowledge of, or participation in, the sprockets conspiracy and provided truthful, full, continuing, and complete cooperation to the Division would receive prison terms or fines in connection with the sprockets conspiracy. *Plus*, in the sentencing hearing for the company's participation in the widgets cartel, the Division would recommend that the court, in calculating XYZ, Inc.'s fine, make a substantial assistance departure that takes into consideration the company's

---

[11] See Question 24 regarding the potential inclusion of specific named former personnel in a corporate leniency agreement.

cooperation in both the widgets and sprockets investigations. The substantial assistance departure that the Division would recommend for XYZ, Inc., therefore, would be greater than if XYZ, Inc. had cooperated in the widgets investigation alone. Consequently, XYZ, Inc. would receive credit for coming forward and cooperating in the sprockets investigation both in terms of obtaining leniency in that matter *and* in terms of receiving a greater reduction in the recommended widgets fine.

9. *How is the substantial assistance for Leniency Plus measured?*

How much credit a company receives for reporting an additional conspiracy depend on a number of factors, including: (1) the strength of the evidence that the cooperating company provides with respect to the leniency investigation; (2) the potential significance of the violation reported in the leniency application, measured in such terms as the volume of commerce involved, the geographic scope, and the number of co-conspirator companies and individuals; and (3) the likelihood that the Division would have uncovered the additional violation without the self-reporting, *e.g.*, if there were little or no overlap in the corporate participants and/or the culpable executives involved in the original cartel under investigation and the Leniency Plus matter, then the credit for the disclosure will be greater. Of these three factors, the first two are given the most weight.[12]

To receive any credit for Leniency Plus at sentencing, the company pleading guilty must also provide truthful, full, continuing, and complete cooperation with the investigation that led to the guilty plea.

10. *What is Penalty Plus?*

Like the Leniency Plus policy described above, the Division's Penalty Plus policy also creates substantial incentives for a company to conduct a thorough internal investigation to detect and report any additional antitrust crimes it uncovers. If a company

---

[12] For a fuller discussion of substantial assistance sentencing departures and the Division's Leniency Plus program, see Brent Snyder, Deputy Assistant Att'y Gen., Antitrust Div., U.S. Dep't of Justice, Individual Accountability for Antitrust Crimes, Speech Before the Yale School of Management Global Antitrust Enforcement Conference (Feb. 19, 2016), https://www.justice.gov/opa/file/826721/download; Bill Baer, Assistant Att'y Gen., Antitrust Div., U.S. Dep't of Justice, Prosecuting Antitrust Crimes, Speech Before Georgetown University Law Center Global Antitrust Enforcement Symposium (Sept. 10, 2014), https://www.justice.gov/atr/file/517741/download; and Scott D. Hammond, Deputy Assistant Att'y Gen., Antitrust Div., U.S. Dep't of Justice, Measuring the Value of Second-In Cooperation in Corporate Plea Negotiations, Speech Before the ABA Antitrust Section 2006 Spring Meeting (March 29, 2006), https://www.justice.gov/atr/file/518436/download.

pleads guilty to an antitrust offense but fails to report an additional antitrust crime it was also involved in, that company not only foregoes potential credit from the Division's Leniency Plus policy, but the Division will generally seek a more severe punishment under its Penalty Plus policy for the additional crime. Under the Penalty Plus policy, if the Division independently uncovers evidence that a company, which previously pleaded guilty to an antitrust crime, was also involved in one or more additional antitrust crimes that it did not report to the Division by the time of the prior guilty plea, then at sentencing for those additional crimes the Division will seek an appropriate sentencing enhancement.

The severity of the Penalty Plus enhancement the Division seeks depends on the reason the company failed to report the additional antitrust crime. If a company conducts an internal investigation and fails to discover the additional antitrust crime but, after the Division discovers that crime, agrees to plead guilty and cooperate with respect to that crime, the Division would begin any downward adjustment for that cooperation from a higher point in the Guidelines range for the additional antitrust crime. The sentencing consequences will be greater for a company that made no meaningful effort to conduct an internal investigation or was aware of the additional antitrust crime but elected not to report. In that case, the Division will seek a more severe Penalty Plus enhancement and will likely recommend that the district court impose probation on the company pursuant to U.S. Sentencing Guidelines §§8D1.1 - 8D1.4.[13]

In the most egregious cases, the Division will recommend that the district court consider the company's failure to report the additional antitrust crime as an aggravating sentencing factor which warrants a fine at the top end of the Guidelines range or an upward departure and a sentence above the Guidelines range. In such cases, the Division may also recommend that the district court appoint an external monitor to ensure that the company develops an appropriate culture of corporate compliance.

11. *If the leniency applicant is a subject or target of, or a defendant in, a separate investigation, will the applicant's conditional leniency letter contain any changes from the model corporate conditional leniency letter?*

Yes. An additional paragraph will be included when necessary in the model corporate conditional leniency letter to make clear that the protection afforded to the company and its executives pursuant to the letter, as well as their cooperation obligations, extend only to the activity reported pursuant to the leniency application and not to the separate investigation. In so doing, the letter will detail the company's acknowledgement of its status and that of its directors, officers, and employees as subjects, targets, or defendants in the separate investigation; the lack of effect of the conditional leniency letter on the ability of the Division to prosecute it and its directors, officers, and employees in that separate investigation; and the lack of effect of the separate

---

[13] The U.S. Sentencing Guidelines are available at http://www.ussc.gov/sites/default/files/pdf/guidelines-manual/2016/GLMFull.pdf.

investigation on the cooperation obligations of the company and its directors, officers, and employees under the conditional leniency letter.[14]

In addition, directors, officers and employees of the applicant who are subjects, targets, or defendants in the separate investigation but who are interviewed by the Division in connection with his or her employer's leniency application will be given a separate letter in which the individual acknowledges his or her status in the separate investigation and acknowledges that the leniency letter governs the conditions of the individual's eligibility for leniency protection with respect to the anticompetitive activity being reported pursuant to the leniency letter.[15]

Meaning of "Discovery of the Illegal Activity"

12. ***Both Type A Leniency and Type B Leniency require that "[t]he corporation, upon its discovery of the illegal activity being reported, took prompt and effective action to terminate its part in the activity." How does the Division interpret "discovery of the illegal activity being reported," especially when high-level officials of the company participated in the cartel?***

Questions have arisen about what it means for the corporation to "discover" the illegal activity being reported. More specifically, in cases (usually involving small, closely held corporations) where the top executives, board members, or owners participated in the conspiracy, it has been suggested that the corporation may not be eligible for leniency because the corporation's "discovery" of the activity arguably occurred when those participants joined the conspiracy.

The Division, however, generally considers the corporation to have discovered the illegal activity at the earliest date on which either the board of directors or counsel for the corporation (either inside or outside) was first informed of the conduct at issue. Thus, the fact that top executives, individual board members, or owners participated in the conspiracy does not necessarily bar the corporation from eligibility for leniency. The purpose of this interpretation is to ensure that as soon as the authoritative representatives of the company for legal matters—the board or counsel representing the corporation—are advised of the illegal activity, they take action to cease that activity. In the case of a small, closely held corporation in which the board of directors is never formally advised of the activity, because all members of the board are conspirators, the corporation still may qualify under this provision if the activity is terminated promptly after legal counsel is first informed of the activity.

---

[14] A copy of the Model Dual Investigations Leniency Letter is available at https://www.justice.gov/atr/leniency-program.

[15] A copy of the Model Dual Investigations Acknowledgement Letter for Employees is available at https://www.justice.gov/atr/leniency-program.

13. *Does the grant of conditional leniency always cover activity up until the date of the conditional leniency letter?*

The grant of conditional leniency usually protects the applicant for any activity committed in furtherance of a criminal antitrust violation prior to the date of the conditional leniency letter. This is because, in the vast majority of cases, leniency applicants approach the Division promptly after discovery of the anticompetitive activity in order to enhance the likelihood that they are the first applicant and that a co-conspirator or an employee does not beat them in the race to obtain leniency. In such cases, paragraph 3 of the Division's model corporate conditional leniency letter provides that "[T]he Antitrust Division agrees not to bring any criminal prosecution against Applicant for any act or offense it may have committed prior to the date of this letter in furtherance of the anticompetitive activity being reported." The introductory paragraph in the model leniency letters defines "date of this letter" as the date that the Division executes the conditional leniency letter.

In rare cases, leniency applicants do not approach the Division until a significant period of time has lapsed since discovery of the anticompetitive activity being reported. In such instances, there can be a significant lapse in time between the date the applicant discovered the conspiracy—and was required to take prompt and effective action to terminate its participation —and the date the applicant reported the activity to the Division. In these cases, the Division reserves the right to grant conditional leniency only up to the date the applicant represents that it terminated its participation in the activity. The Division will also likely insist on including both a discovery date and a termination date in paragraph 1 of the corporate conditional leniency letter. The discovery date and termination date representations would be that the applicant "discovered the anticompetitive activity being reported in or about [month/year] and terminated its participation in the activity in or about [month/year]."[16] The applicant bears the burden of proving the accuracy of these representations.[17]

---

[16] *See* Model Corp. Conditional Leniency Letter n.3.

[17] *Id.* ¶ 1 ("Applicant agrees that it bears the burden of proving its eligibility to receive leniency, including the accuracy of the representations made in this paragraph and that it fully understands the consequences that might result from a revocation of leniency as explained in paragraph 3 of this Agreement.") The applicant, as the party seeking leniency and representing that it is eligible, has the burden of establishing its eligibility for leniency.

Termination of Participation in Anticompetitive Activity

14. *What constitutes "prompt and effective action to terminate [the applicant's] participation in the anticompetitive activity being reported upon discovery of the activity?"*

The model corporate conditional leniency letter requires that a leniency applicant promptly terminated its participation in the anticompetitive activity being reported upon its discovery of the illegal conduct.[18] This prerequisite to obtaining leniency exists because, as a matter of good public policy, the Division does not believe that it would be appropriate to provide leniency to a company that discovers illegal conduct but then elects to continue engaging in that conduct. What constitutes prompt and effective action will, of course, depend on the particular circumstances in each leniency matter. A primary consideration is what steps are taken by management in response to the discovery of the anticompetitive activity being reported. For example, a company must not use managers or executives who were involved in the anticompetitive activity to investigate the activity, to formulate the company's response to the discovery of such activity, or to determine the appropriate disciplinary action against employees who participated in the activity. Other considerations are the size of the applicant corporation, its corporate structure, the complexity of its operations involved in the reported activity (including its geographic scope), and the nature of the reported activity.

A company terminates its part in anticompetitive activity by stopping any further participation in that activity, unless continued participation is with Division approval in order to assist the Division in its investigation. The Division will not disqualify a leniency applicant whose illegal conduct ended promptly after it was discovered merely because the applicant did not take some particular action. Moreover, as an exercise of prosecutorial discretion, if the Division is persuaded that the company and its high-level management had done everything that could reasonably be expected of them to terminate the company's involvement in the anticompetitive activity being reported, the Division would not revoke a company's conditional acceptance into the Leniency Program because a lower-level employee in one of the company's remote offices continued for some short period of time to have conspiratorial contacts with his or her counterpart. On the other hand, if any of the applicant's executives or high-level managers who were members of the conspiracy prior to discovery, continue to act in furtherance of the conspiracy despite that company's remedial actions, then the company should recognize that the Division may decide that the applicant did not promptly and effectively end its participation in the conspiracy.

---

[18] *Id.* ("Applicant represents . . . that . . . it . . . took prompt and effective action to terminate its participation in the anticompetitive activity being reported upon discovery of the activity.")

A company that seeks a marker from the Division immediately after discovering anticompetitive activity, and that effectively terminates its involvement in that activity at about the same time, will be viewed by the Division as having taken prompt and effective action. To date, almost every company that has sought leniency from the Division has done so shortly after discovering the anticompetitive activity being reported. On the other hand, an applicant that discovers anticompetitive activity, but, instead of reporting it to the Division, keeps the culpable employees in the same positions with no repercussions or inadequate supervision, and fails to prevent those employees from continuing to engage in the anticompetitive activity, can expect the Division to decline to grant it leniency. As with the discovery representation, the applicant has the burden of proving that it took prompt and effective action, and will not receive final leniency unless it satisfies its burden of proof.[19]

Leniency applicants most commonly effectuate termination by reporting the anticompetitive activity to the Division and refraining from further participation—unless continued participation is with Division approval. Applicants may be asked to assist the Division with a covert investigation; for example, by participating in consensually monitored discussions with other members of the conspiracy.[20] Whether the Division's investigation is overt or covert, however, there is a risk of obstruction resulting from unauthorized disclosures about the application or the investigation. Therefore, at the outset of the leniency application, the applicant should discuss with Division staff who within the company it can tell about the leniency application, as well as when and how to inform them.

Not the Leader or Originator of the Activity

Part A of the Corporate Leniency Policy, section A6, requires that "[t]he corporation did not coerce another party to participate in the illegal activity and clearly was not the leader in, or originator of, the activity." Similarly, Part B of the Corporate Leniency Policy, section B7, requires that:

> The Division determine[] that granting leniency would not be unfair to others, considering the nature of the illegal activity, the confessing corporation's role in it, and when the corporation comes forward.

The model corporate conditional leniency letter incorporates this requirement in paragraph 1, which requires the applicant to represent that it "did not coerce any other party to participate in the anticompetitive activity being reported and was not the leader

---

[19] *Id.* (see introductory paragraph and paragraph 1).

[20] When an applicant's employees are participating in cartel meetings and communications at the direction of the Division to assist with a covert investigation, the employees are deemed to be agents of the Division under U.S. law and are no longer deemed co-conspirators.

in, or the originator of, the activity." As with the discovery and termination representations, the applicant bears the burden of proving the accuracy of this representation.[21]

15. *How does the Division define what it means to be "the leader in, or originator of, the activity"?*

The Corporate Leniency Policy refers to "*the* leader" and "*the* originator of the activity," rather than "*a*" leader or "*an*" originator. Applicants are disqualified from obtaining leniency on this ground only if they were clearly the single organizer or single ringleader of a conspiracy. If, for example, there are two ringleaders in a five-firm conspiracy, then all of the firms, including the two leaders, are potentially eligible for leniency. Or, if in a two-firm conspiracy, each firm played a decisive role in the operation of the cartel, either firm is potentially eligible for leniency. In addition, an applicant will not be disqualified under this condition just because it is the largest company in the industry or has the greatest market share if it was not clearly the single organizer or single ringleader of the conspiracy. Exclusion under the condition is rare and wherever possible, the Division has construed or interpreted its program in favor of accepting an applicant into the Leniency Program in order to provide the maximum amount of incentives and opportunities for companies to come forward and report their illegal activity.

Cooperation Obligations

16. *What are the corporate applicant's cooperation obligations?*

Type A Leniency requires that "[t]he corporation reports the wrongdoing with candor and completeness and provides full, continuing and complete cooperation to the Division throughout the investigation." Type B Leniency requires that "[t]he corporation reports the wrongdoing with candor and completeness and provides full, continuing and complete cooperation that advances the Division in its investigation." Both Type A and Type B Leniency require that "[t]he confession of wrongdoing is truly a corporate act, as opposed to isolated confessions of individual executives or officials." Paragraph 2 of the model corporate conditional leniency letter describes specific cooperation obligations of the applicant, such as providing documents, information, and materials wherever located; using its best efforts to secure the cooperation of its current directors, officers, and employees;[22] and paying restitution to victims.

---

[21] *See* Model Corp. Conditional Leniency Letter ¶ 1.

[22] In specific cases, the Division, in its discretion, may also agree to cover specific named former employees, as discussed in Question 24.

17. *As part of the applicant's cooperation obligations, will the applicant be required to provide communications or documents protected by the attorney-client privilege or work-product doctrine?*

Paragraphs 2 and 4 of the model corporate conditional leniency letter state that the applicant and its directors, officers, and employees are not required to produce communications or documents protected by the attorney-client privilege or work-product doctrine as part of their cooperation. Moreover, as stated in the introductory paragraph of the model corporate conditional leniency letter, the Division does not consider disclosures made by counsel in furtherance of the leniency application to constitute a waiver of the attorney-client privilege or the work-product protection. While the Division does not require or request the production of communications or documents protected by the attorney-client privilege or work-product doctrine, and does not refuse to grant leniency because a corporation has not produced such protected information, some corporations, after consulting counsel, conclude that a voluntary disclosure of such protected communications and/or documents is in the best interest of the corporation.

Effect of Refusal of Individual Executives to Cooperate

18. *If one or more individual corporate executives refuse to cooperate, will the corporate applicant be barred from leniency on the basis that the confession is no longer a "corporate act" or that the corporation is not providing "truthful, full, continuing, and complete" cooperation?*

In order for the confession of wrongdoing to be a "corporate act" and in order for the cooperation to be considered "truthful, full, continuing, and complete," the corporation must, in the Division's judgment, be taking all legal, reasonable steps to cooperate with the Division's investigation. The model corporate conditional leniency letter requires the company to use "its best efforts to secure the truthful, full, continuing, and complete cooperation" of its current directors, officers, and employees excluding any current personnel who are carved out of the letter. In those cases where the conditional leniency letter's cooperation requirements and leniency protections also cover specific named former directors, officers, or employees, the company is also required to use its best efforts to secure those individuals' cooperation. If the corporation is unable to secure such cooperation of one or more individuals, then that would not necessarily prevent the Division from granting the leniency application. However, the number and significance of the individuals who fail to cooperate, and the steps taken by the company to secure their cooperation, would be relevant to the Division's determinations of whether there is a corporate confession, whether the corporation's cooperation is truly "truthful, full, continuing, and complete," and whether the Division is receiving the benefit of the bargain if certain key executives are not cooperating. Of course, in such situations, the non-cooperating individuals would lose the protection given to cooperating employees under the corporate conditional leniency letter, and the Division would be free to prosecute such individuals for the antitrust crime and any related offenses.

Restitution

19. *What is the meaning of the qualifier in the Corporate Leniency Policy that states "[w]here possible, the corporation makes restitution to injured parties"?*

There is a strong presumption in favor of requiring restitution in leniency situations. Restitution is excused only where, as a practical matter, it is not possible. Examples of situations in which an applicant might be excused from making restitution include situations where the applicant is in bankruptcy and is prohibited by court order from undertaking additional obligations, or where there was only one victim of the conspiracy and it is now defunct. Another example of a situation where the Division will not require the applicant to pay full restitution is if doing so will substantially jeopardize the organization's continued viability. Paragraph 2(g) of the model corporate conditional leniency letter requires that the applicant make "all reasonable efforts, to the satisfaction of the Antitrust Division, to pay restitution." Thus, the applicant must demonstrate to the Division that it has satisfied its obligation to pay restitution before it will be granted final leniency. Restitution is normally resolved through civil actions with private plaintiffs. The Antitrust Criminal Penalty Enhancement and Reform Act of 2004, also referred to as ACPERA,[23] limits the liability for civil damages claims in private state or federal antitrust actions for a qualifying leniency applicant. For claims against a corporation that enters into an antitrust leniency agreement with the Division or a cooperating individual covered by such an agreement, a claimant cannot recover damages exceeding the "portion of the actual damages sustained by such claimant which is attributable to the commerce done by the applicant in the goods or services affected by the violation."[24] To qualify for this limitation, the corporation or cooperating individuals must meet the conditions of the Corporate Leniency Policy, including cooperating fully with the Division's investigation, and must meet certain requirements in connection with the claimant's civil action, including providing the claimant with a full account of all potentially relevant facts known to the corporation or cooperating individual and all potentially relevant documents.

---

[23] Pub. L. No. 108-237, Title II, §§ 211 to 214, 118 Stat. 661, 666-68 (2004), as amended Pub. L. No. 111-30, § 2, 123 Stat. 1775 (2009) and Pub. L. No. 111-190, §§ 1 to 4, 124 Stat. 1275, 1275-76 (2010) (set out as a note under 15 U.S.C. § 1).

[24] ACPERA § 213(a).

20. *What are the applicant's restitution obligations for injuries caused by the effects of the anticompetitive activity being reported on foreign commerce?*

The model corporate conditional leniency letter reflects the holdings of the Supreme Court and the courts of appeals that damages for violations of the Sherman Act do not include foreign effects independent of and not proximately caused by any adverse effect on U.S. commerce.[25] Accordingly, paragraph 2(g) of the model corporate conditional leniency letter states: "However, Applicant is not required to pay restitution to victims whose antitrust injuries are independent of, and not proximately caused by, any effect on (i) trade or commerce within the United States, (ii) import trade or commerce, or (iii) the export trade or commerce of a person engaged in such trade or commerce in the United States, which effect was proximately caused by the anticompetitive activity being reported."

21. *What are the applicant's restitution obligations if the Division ultimately brings no criminal case?*

In certain cases where a corporation has otherwise met the requirements for leniency and has agreed to pay restitution, the Division may ultimately determine that either: (1) the leniency applicant has not engaged in any criminal antitrust conduct; or (2) even though the leniency applicant has engaged in criminal antitrust conduct, prosecution of the other conspiracy participants is not justified under the Principles of Federal Prosecution given the weakness of the evidence or other problems with the case. The issue has arisen as to whether, in such cases, the leniency applicant still has to pay restitution as agreed in the corporate conditional leniency letter.

If the Division's investigation ultimately reveals that the leniency applicant has not engaged in any criminal antitrust conduct, the Division will not grant leniency because it is unnecessary. Obligations placed on the applicant by the Corporate Leniency Policy or the applicant's conditional leniency letter with the Division no longer apply once the Division determines there is no underlying criminal antitrust conduct. In such cases, the Division will so advise the applicant in writing and the applicant will have no duty to pay restitution. If the leniency applicant has already paid restitution or is in the process of doing so, the applicant must resolve the matter with the recipient. Once the Division decides not to grant leniency, the applicant has no duty toward the Division, nor does the Division have any duty to help "reverse" any steps taken by the applicant to make restitution. Due to the Division's use of a marker system, however, this situation is not likely to occur. Through the marker system, the applicant has the opportunity to conduct a thorough internal investigation and the Division has the opportunity to

---

[25] *See F. Hoffmann-La Roche Ltd. v. Empagran S.A.*, 542 U.S. 155 (2004); *Lotes Co., Ltd. v. Hon Hai Precision Indus. Co.*, 753 F.3d 395 (2d Cir. 2014); *In re Dynamic Random Access Memory (DRAM) Antitrust Litig.*, 546 F.3d 981 (9th Cir. 2008); *In re Monosodium Glutamate Antitrust Litig.*, 477 F.3d 535 (8th Cir. 2007); *Empagran S.A. v. F. Hoffmann-La Roche Ltd.*, 417 F.3d 1267 (D.C. Cir. 2005).

interview key corporate executives before a conditional leniency letter is issued. Thus, any issues regarding whether a criminal antitrust violation occurred should be resolved during the marker stage.

If, on the other hand, the Division concludes that the leniency applicant has engaged in criminal antitrust activity and conditionally grants the leniency application, but later closes the investigation without charging any other entity in the conspiracy, the obligation to pay restitution will remain in effect. In such a case, the Division will notify the leniency applicant and the subjects of the investigation in writing that the investigation has been closed. In such cases, the leniency applicant may withdraw its application if it so chooses, and, if it does, the obligations undertaken by the applicant pursuant to the conditional leniency letter—including the payment of restitution—will no longer be in effect. If the applicant withdraws its application, the Division, for its part, will technically no longer be prohibited from prosecuting the applicant and will not provide any additional assurances of nonprosecution. Again, the Division will not assist in restoring any restitution already paid if the leniency application is withdrawn. Moreover, if the applicant chooses to withdraw its leniency application, it will not qualify for detrebling of civil damages under the Antitrust Criminal Penalty Enhancement and Reform Act of 2004. Also, once an applicant has fulfilled all of the conditions for leniency and the Division has issued a final leniency letter, the Division does not permit the leniency recipient to withdraw its leniency application.

Leniency for Corporate Directors, Officers, and Employees

22. *What are the conditions for leniency protection for the applicant's current directors, officers, and employees?*

If a corporation qualifies for Type A Leniency, all current directors, officers, and employees of the corporation who admit their involvement in the criminal antitrust violation as part of the corporate confession will also receive leniency if they admit their wrongdoing with candor and completeness and continue to assist the Division throughout the investigation. In addition, the applicant's current directors, officers, and employees who did not participate in the conspiracy but who had knowledge of the conspiracy and cooperate with the Division are also included in the scope of the conditional leniency letter, as explained below. If a current director, officer, or employee does not fully cooperate with the Division's investigation, he or she will be excluded from, or "carved out" of, the conditional leniency letter. Also, as discussed below, if a current director, officer, or employee fully cooperates with the Division's investigation before the conditional leniency letter is issued, but stops fully cooperating after the letter is issued, then that individual's protections under the corporate conditional leniency letter are void and the Division may notify that individual that his or her protection under the letter is revoked. As discussed in Question 24 below, the Division may also exercise its discretion to include in the scope of the conditional leniency letter the names of specific former directors, officers, and employees of the corporation.

If a corporation qualifies for Type B Leniency, the Corporate Leniency Policy states that individuals who come forward with the corporation will still be considered for immunity from criminal prosecution on the same basis as if they had approached the Division individually. Thus, the Division has more discretion with respect to personnel of Type B Leniency applicants. The Division often chooses to include protection for current directors, officers, and employees of Type B Leniency applicants. However, the Division may exercise its discretion to exclude from the protections that the conditional leniency letter offers those current directors, officers, and employees who are determined to be highly culpable. As discussed in Question 24 below, the Division may also exercise its discretion to include in the scope of a Type B corporate conditional leniency letter specific named former directors, officers, and employees of the corporation.

Leniency must be fully earned. Paragraph 4 of the corporate conditional leniency letter details the specific conditions of leniency for the applicant's directors, officers, and employees who had knowledge of, or participated in, the anticompetitive activity being reported by the applicant. The conditions are: (1) verification of the applicant's representations in paragraph 1 of the corporate conditional leniency letter; (2) the applicant's truthful, full, continuing, and complete cooperation as defined in paragraph 2 of the corporate conditional leniency letter; (3) admission by the pertinent director, officer, or employee of his or her knowledge of, or participation in, the anticompetitive activity being reported; and (4) the individual's truthful, full, continuing, and complete cooperation with the Division in its investigation and resulting prosecutions. The specific cooperation obligations of the individuals are also defined in paragraph 4 of the corporate conditional leniency letter, such as the provision of documents, records and other materials and information; participation in interviews; and the provision of testimony.

As noted below, the Division reserves the right to revoke the conditional protections of the corporate conditional leniency letter with respect to any director, officer, or employee who failed to comply fully with his or her obligations under the letter, who the Division determines caused the corporate applicant to be ineligible for leniency, who continued to participate in the anticompetitive activity being reported after the corporation took action to terminate its participation in the anticompetitive activity and notified the individual to cease his or her participation in the anticompetitive activity, or who obstructed or attempted to obstruct an investigation of the anticompetitive activity at any time, whether the obstruction occurred before or after the date of the corporate conditional leniency letter.[26]

---

[26] This issue is discussed further at Question 30 and addressed in paragraph 4 of the model corporate conditional leniency letter.

Definition of Current Employees

23. *How is "current director, officer, or employee" defined for purposes of the cooperation obligations and leniency protection of the corporate conditional leniency letter?*

Status as a "current director, officer, or employee" is defined at the time the corporate conditional leniency letter is signed by the Division. Thus, leniency for individuals who are directors, officers, and employees of the applicant at the time the letter is signed by the Division will continue after they leave their employment so long as they satisfy their obligations under the corporate conditional leniency letter.

Leniency for Former Employees

24. *Can an applicant's former directors, officers, and employees be included in the scope of the conditional leniency letter?*

Former directors, officers, and employees are presumptively excluded from any grant of corporate leniency. The Corporate Leniency Policy does not refer to former directors, officers, or employees. The Division is under no obligation to extend leniency to former directors, officers, or employees.

At the Division's sole discretion, specific, named former directors, officers, or employees may receive nonprosecution protection under a corporate conditional leniency letter or by a separate nonprosecution agreement. Such protections are only offered when these specific former directors, officers, or employees provide substantial, noncumulative cooperation against remaining potential targets, or when their cooperation is necessary for the leniency applicant to make a confession of criminal antitrust activity sufficient to be eligible for conditional leniency.[27] In these circumstances, such decisions are made on an individualized, case-by-case basis, consistent with the Principles of Federal Prosecution. Former directors, officers, and employees must provide truthful, full, continuing and complete cooperation to the Division throughout its investigation and resulting prosecutions.

III. Criteria under the Leniency Policy for Individuals

25. *What are the criteria for leniency under the Leniency Policy for Individuals?*

An individual who approaches the Division on his or her own behalf to report illegal antitrust activity may qualify for leniency under the Leniency Policy for Individuals. As with a corporate applicant, an individual leniency applicant is required to

---

[27] See Question 5.

admit to his or her participation in a criminal antitrust violation.[28] The individual must not have approached the Division previously as part of a corporate approach seeking leniency for the same conduct. Once a corporation attempts to qualify for leniency under the Corporate Leniency Policy, current directors, officers, and employees who come forward and admit their involvement in the criminal antitrust violation as part of the corporate confession will be considered for leniency under the provisions of the Corporate Leniency Policy. No current or former directors, officers, or employees of a company that has applied for leniency under the Corporate Leniency Policy may be considered for leniency under the Leniency Policy for Individuals.

Leniency will be granted to an individual reporting illegal antitrust activity before an investigation has begun if the following three conditions are met:[29]

(1) At the time the individual comes forward to report the activity, the Division has not received information about the activity being reported from any other source.

(2) The individual reports the wrongdoing with candor and completeness and provides full, continuing, and complete cooperation to the Division throughout the investigation.

(3) The individual did not coerce another party to participate in the activity and clearly was not the leader in, or the originator of, the activity.

Any individual who does not qualify for leniency under the Corporate Leniency Policy or Leniency Policy for Individuals may still be considered for statutory or informal immunity.

---

[28] See also the discussion at Question 6 regarding the Division's policy concerning coverage of non-antitrust crimes, which applies to individual leniency applicants as well as to corporate applicants.

[29] As with the model corporate conditional leniency letter, the model individual conditional leniency letter provides that the leniency protection applies to "any act or offense [the applicant] may have committed prior to the date of this letter in furtherance of the anticompetitive activity being reported." Model Individual Conditional Leniency Letter ¶ 3. With respect to an individual leniency applicant, if a significant lapse in time occurs between the applicant's termination of his or her participation in the anticompetitive activity being reported and the date the applicant reported the activity to the Division, the Division reserves the right to grant conditional leniency only up to the date the applicant terminated his or her participation in the activity. Model Individual Conditional Leniency Letter n.2.

Paragraph 2 of the model individual conditional leniency letter describes specific cooperation obligations of the individual applicant, such as the production of documents, records, and other materials and information; participation in interviews; and provision of testimony. As is the case with a corporate applicant, an individual applicant is not required, and will not be asked, to produce communications or documents protected under the attorney-client privilege or work-product doctrine.[30]

Regarding the leadership condition, an individual leniency applicant is required to represent in his or her leniency letter that, "in connection with the anticompetitive activity being reported, [he/she] did not coerce any other party to participate in the activity and was not the leader in, or the originator of, the activity" in order to establish his or her eligibility for leniency. The applicant bears the burden of proving the accuracy of this representation.[31] As with a corporate applicant, an individual applicant would only be disqualified from obtaining leniency based on leadership role if he or she is clearly the single organizer or single ringleader of a conspiracy. Accordingly, in situations where individual conspirators are viewed as co-equals or where there are two or more individual conspirators that are viewed as leaders or originators, any of the participants are potentially eligible for leniency under the Leniency Policy for Individuals.

IV. The Conditional Leniency Letter

26. *What is the conditional leniency letter, and why is it conditional?*

The conditional leniency letter is the initial leniency letter given to a leniency applicant. The Division has a model corporate conditional leniency letter and a model individual conditional leniency letter.[32] The initial grant of leniency pursuant to the letters is conditional because a final grant of leniency depends upon the applicant performing certain obligations over the course of the criminal investigation and any resulting prosecution of co-conspirators, such as: establishment of its eligibility; its truthful, full, continuing, and complete cooperation; and its payment of restitution to victims, as set forth in the letter. The final grant of leniency also depends on the Division

---

[30] Model Individual Conditional Leniency Letter ¶ 2(a), (d). As with a corporate applicant, an individual, after consulting with counsel, may conclude that a voluntary disclosure of such privileged communications or documents is in his or her best interest.

[31] Model Individual Conditional Leniency Letter ¶ 1 ("Applicant agrees that [he/she] bears the burden of proving [his/her] eligibility to receive leniency, including the accuracy of the representations made in this paragraph, and that [he/she] fully understands the consequences that might result from a revocation of leniency as explained in paragraph 3 of this Agreement.").

[32] Both model conditional letters are available at https://www.justice.gov/atr/leniency-program.

verifying the applicant's representations regarding its eligibility. Only those who qualify for leniency should receive its rewards. After all of the applicant's obligations have been satisfied (usually after the investigation and prosecution of co-conspirators have been concluded) and the Division has verified the applicant's representations regarding eligibility, the Division will issue the applicant a final leniency letter confirming that the conditions of the conditional leniency letter have been satisfied and that the leniency application has been granted.

The conditional nature of the leniency initially granted is reflected in the model leniency letters. The introductory paragraph of the model corporate and individual conditional leniency letters states that the agreement "is conditional." Further, the letters state in paragraph 3 that, "[s]ubject to verification of Applicant's representations in paragraph 1 above, and subject to [its/Applicant's] truthful, full, continuing, and complete cooperation, as described in paragraph 2 above, the Antitrust Division agrees conditionally to accept Applicant into [Part A/Part B of the Corporate Leniency Program/the Individual Leniency Program]." The letters also state in the introductory paragraph that the agreement "depends upon Applicant (1) establishing that [it/he or she] is eligible for leniency as [it/he or she] represents in paragraph 1 of [the] Agreement, and (2) cooperating in the Antitrust Division's investigation as required by paragraph 2 of [the] Agreement." As noted above, the applicant, as the party seeking leniency, has the burden of establishing its eligibility for leniency.[33] The introductory paragraph further notes that, "[a]fter Applicant establishes that [it/he or she] is eligible to receive leniency and provides the required cooperation, the Antitrust Division will notify Applicant in writing that [it/he or she] has been granted unconditional leniency."

Although many of the leniency requirements are fulfilled during the criminal investigation, the Division understands that applicants want assurances up front, even if conditional, that they will receive nonprosecution protection at the conclusion of the investigation if they fulfill the requirements of the Leniency Program. The Division's conditional leniency letters address that need. In contrast, many voluntary disclosure programs of other prosecuting agencies do not provide any upfront assurances regarding nonprosecution. Thus, the alternative to the conditional letter would be for the Division to give no assurances until the conclusion of the investigation and prosecution of co-conspirators. The conditional leniency letters, however, provide companies and their executives with a transparent and predictable disclosure program, and have been very effective both for the Division in setting forth the requirements of leniency and for applicants in meeting those requirements.

---

[33] *See supra* note 17.

V. Potential Revocation of Conditional Leniency and the Final Unconditional Leniency Letter

27. *Under what circumstances can the Division revoke an applicant's conditional leniency, and will the Division provide the applicant with any advance notice of a staff recommendation to revoke conditional leniency?*

If the Division determines, before it grants an applicant a final, unconditional leniency letter, that the applicant "(1) contrary to [its/his/her] representations in paragraph 1 of [the conditional leniency letter], is not eligible for leniency or (2) has not provided the cooperation required by paragraph 2 of [the conditional leniency letter]," the Division may revoke the applicant's conditional acceptance into the Leniency Program.[34] Before the Division makes a final determination to revoke a corporate applicant's conditional leniency, it will notify applicant's counsel in writing of staff's recommendation to revoke the leniency and provide counsel with an opportunity to meet with the staff, the Criminal DAAG, and the Director of Criminal Enforcement regarding the revocation.[35] During the time that a recommendation to revoke an applicant's leniency is under consideration, the Division will suspend the applicant's obligation to cooperate so that the applicant is not put in the position of continuing to provide evidence that could be used against it should the conditional leniency be revoked. In the history of the Division's Leniency Program, the Division has revoked only one conditional leniency letter out of the more than 200 conditional leniency letters issued.

28. *When can an applicant or its employees judicially challenge a Division decision to revoke conditional leniency?*

Paragraph 3 of the model corporate and individual conditional leniency letters states that the applicant "understands that the Antitrust Division's Leniency Program is an exercise of the Division's prosecutorial discretion, and [it/he/she] agrees that [it/he/she] may not, and will not, seek judicial review of any Division decision to revoke [its/his/her] conditional leniency unless and until [it/he/she] has been charged by indictment or information for engaging in the anticompetitive activity being reported." Paragraph 4 of the model corporate conditional leniency letter also notes that "[j]udicial review of any Antitrust Division decision to revoke [an individual's] conditional nonprosecution protection granted [under the corporate conditional leniency letter] is not available unless and until the individual has been charged by indictment or information." The Division's Leniency Program is an exercise of prosecutorial discretion generally not

---

[34] Model Corp. Conditional Leniency Letter ¶ 3; Model Individual Conditional Leniency Letter ¶ 3.

[35] Model Corp. Conditional Leniency Letter ¶ 3. The individual conditional leniency letter provides that this notice will be given absent exigent circumstances, such as risk of flight. Model Individual Conditional Leniency Letter ¶ 3.

subject to judicial review. Accordingly, the proper avenue to challenge a revocation of a leniency letter is to raise the letter as a defense post-indictment.[36]

29. *If a corporate conditional leniency letter is revoked, what will happen to the protection provided in the letter for the corporation's directors, officers, and employees?*

If before granting the applicant unconditional leniency the Division determines that the applicant is not eligible for leniency or has not provided the required cooperation, the conditional leniency agreement "shall be void" and the Division may revoke the applicant's conditional acceptance into the Leniency Program.[37] Thus, the protection provided to employees pursuant to the letter no longer exists. However, as a matter of prosecutorial discretion, even if the Division revokes a company's conditional leniency letter, the Division will elect not to prosecute individual employees, so long as they had provided truthful, full, continuing, and complete cooperation to the Division prior to the revocation and, in the Division's view, were not responsible for the revocation.

30. *Under what circumstances can the protection granted to an individual under a corporate conditional leniency letter be revoked?*

As noted in the model corporate conditional leniency letter, if a director, officer, or employee who is included in the scope of the leniency letter fails to comply fully with his or her obligations under the letter, the Division may revoke any conditional leniency, immunity, or nonprosecution granted to the individual under the letter.[38] The Division also reserves the right to revoke the conditional nonprosecution protections of the corporate conditional leniency letter with respect to any director, officer, or employee who the Division determines caused the corporate applicant to be ineligible for leniency under paragraph 1 of the corporate conditional leniency letter, who continued to participate in the anticompetitive activity being reported after the corporation took action to terminate its participation in the activity and notified the individual to cease his or her participation in the activity,[39] or who obstructed or attempted to obstruct an investigation

---

[36] *Stolt-Nielsen, S.A. v. United States*, 442 F.3d 177, 183-187 (3d Cir. 2006).

[37] Model Corp. Conditional Leniency Letter ¶ 3.

[38] Model Corp. Conditional Leniency Letter ¶ 4.

[39] Such notice ordinarily is part of the corporation's prompt and effective action to terminate its participation in the anticompetitive activity being reported. It need not be specific to the individual or the individual's particular conduct so long as it reasonably notifies the director, officer, or employee that he or she should not participate in the illegal activity. General instructions or guidance by the corporation not to engage in cartel or illegal conduct generally, made prior to the corporation's discovery of the

of the anticompetitive activity at any time, whether the obstruction occurred before or after the date of the corporate conditional leniency letter.[40]

31. *What notice or process will be given to an individual if the Division is contemplating revoking his or her conditional protections provided in a corporate conditional leniency letter?*

Absent exigent circumstances, such as risk of flight, before the Division makes a final determination to revoke an individual's conditional leniency, immunity, or nonprosecution provided under a corporate conditional leniency letter, it will notify in writing the individual (or his or her counsel, if represented) and the corporate applicant's counsel of staff's recommendation to revoke the protections provided in the letter and provide an opportunity to meet with the staff, the Criminal DAAG, and the Director of Criminal Enforcement regarding the revocation.[41] During the time that a revocation recommendation is under consideration, the Division will suspend the individual's obligation to cooperate so that the individual is not put in the position of continuing to provide evidence that could be used against him or her should his or her conditional protections be revoked. If the Division revokes conditional leniency, immunity, or nonprosecution granted to a director, officer, or employee of a corporate applicant, the Division may use against such individual any evidence provided at any time pursuant to the corporate conditional leniency letter by the corporate applicant, the individual, or other directors, officers, or employees of the applicant.[42]

32. *How and when does an applicant receive a final, unconditional leniency letter?*

As noted above and in the model corporate and individual conditional leniency letters, after the applicant "establishes that [it/he/she] is eligible to receive leniency," as represented in paragraph 1 of the conditional leniency letter, "and provides the required cooperation," as set forth in paragraph 2 of the conditional leniency letter, "the Antitrust Division will notify Applicant in writing that [it/he/she] has been granted unconditional leniency."[43] Normally this would occur after the investigation and any resulting prosecutions of the applicant's co-conspirators are completed.

---

anticompetitive activity being reported, does not constitute such notice for purposes of this provision.

[40] Model Corp. Conditional Leniency Letter ¶ 4.

[41] *Id.*

[42] *Id.*

[43] See the introductory paragraphs in the model corporate and individual conditional leniency letters.

VI. Confidentiality

33. *What confidentiality assurances are given to leniency applicants?*

The Division holds the identity of leniency applicants and the information they provide in strict confidence, much like the treatment afforded to confidential informants. Therefore, the Division does not publicly disclose the identity of a leniency applicant or information provided by the applicant, absent prior disclosure by, or agreement with, the applicant, unless required to do so by court order in connection with litigation.

34. *Will the Division disclose information from a leniency applicant to a foreign government?*

The Leniency Program has been the Division's most effective generator of international cartel prosecutions. Invariably, however, when a company is considering whether to report its involvement in international cartel activity, a concern is raised as to whether the Division will be free to disclose the information to any foreign governments in accordance with its obligations under bilateral antitrust cooperation agreements. As noted above, the Division's policy is to treat the identity of, and information provided by, leniency applicants as a confidential matter, much like the treatment afforded to confidential informants. Moreover, the Division has an interest in maximizing the incentives for companies to come forward and self-report antitrust offenses. In that vein, it would create a strong disincentive to self-report and cooperate if a company believed that its self-reporting would result in investigations in other countries and that its cooperation—in the form of admissions, documents, employee statements, and witness identities—would be provided to foreign authorities pursuant to antitrust cooperation agreements, and then possibly used against the company.

While the Division has been at the forefront in advocacy and actions to enhance international cartel enforcement, and the Division has received substantial assistance from foreign governments in obtaining foreign-located evidence in a number of cases, in the final analysis, the Division's overriding interest in protecting the viability of the Leniency Program has resulted in a policy of not disclosing to foreign antitrust agencies information obtained from a leniency applicant unless the leniency applicant agrees first to the disclosure. This aspect of the Division's leniency nondisclosure policy will not insulate the leniency applicant from proceedings in other countries. But it will ensure that cooperation provided by a leniency applicant will not be disclosed by the Division to its foreign counterparts pursuant to antitrust cooperation agreements without the prior consent of the leniency applicant. The Division first announced this policy in 1999, and it is the Division's understanding that virtually every other jurisdiction that has considered the issue has adopted a similar policy.

www.ingramcontent.com/pod-product-compliance
Lightning Source LLC
Chambersburg PA
CBHW081316180526
45170CB00007B/2735